The Blue Man
Poems of the Ordinary

DIANE FURTNEY

FUTURECYCLE PRESS
www.futurecycle.org

Library of Congress Control Number: 2017932590

Published by FutureCycle Press
Lexington, Kentucky, USA

ISBN 978-1-942371-24-3

For J.M.

CONTENTS

THE BLUE MAN

Columbus, Ohio

A crabapple morning. Two rows
of thin-stemmed trees blow

white balloons; down the street
—beside the car at left and right—

they drop in height and disappear
into a Deco skyscraper

downtown. The air is buffed, like the white-
polish paint on the straight

divider lines. Rectangular light
keeps sliding between the trees like lucite

panes. So, who is he? A blond man,
tall, in overalls, ahead on the right-hand

sidewalk, with a circle of a face.
Blue-capped. Around his blue, barrel waist,

a tool belt. In work boots, he saunters
past flower beds circling like colored water

around the trees. Two lines on his face
cup the sides of his mouth, like an embrace.

He could, thoroughly, be
what he appears to be,

Uncle Wonderful, good friend
of Tootle and the Color Kittens,

whose affidavits are not easily
obtained. But the sidewalk breezily

blurs under the leaves a little,
the curb and concrete mottle,

and those might not be smile lines.
They could be the curved, ecliptic plane

on which bitterness is in orbit.
Obsequious, devious, stout,

he could be Snarler,
the bane of wives. Another

toss of blossoms and he's different
—maybe different

with every redoing of the breeze
and light, the ordinary flurries

of which can't be entered twice or even
once, for that matter. Which configuration

you stop on
as your estimation of the blue man

will depend on the slant of your
mental shading, bright or dark-striped over

the trees, with its own history
of moment-to-moment mobilities.

Now he's centered in the mirror. Casual
sunshine bounces off a shoulder buckle

and he's Mr. Fuzzy, Rememberer
of Birthdays. Or someone more familiar—

and letting him go is a minute grief
as well as a same-sized instant of relief,

while the sizes of possibilities
rise and fall and he's

maybe always what he seems to be
now: sweetest guy in the world, trust me.

Twenty to Thirty

SOMETIMES IN ONE'S TWENTIES

San Francisco, 1970s

Coasting out into the open
night: no requirements, no plan,

you're limber and vivid as darkness, and
your shoes, patterned with tan,

aren't scraping your skin,
you're ready, no attention,

no adjustments, are needed: it's end-to-end
lightweight. Not hard to imagine,

though not something you'd mention:
the Background Music of everything, unbroken,

is almost audible. It's fervent
and velvet, the wind, and there's more than

enough of everything for everyone. Even
love might be about to pause in its motion

with a simple turn in your direction.
Of course, nothing has to happen

tonight; you're young, the nights extend
into every distance with no end...

But at a six-streeted corner all of a sudden
an invisible bird tweets; call it a wren,

purple-checked, newly arrived from the Garden
District of the moon; and

there's this fit of mind to body as the body bends
to the world, surely something also bends

this way in the commotion,
is about to encircle...portends...

THE CLAVORIS

Noticing, near the hall, that a section
of the living-room floor was open

(this in San Francisco,
where I'd just pushed open my studio's

French doors), what was clearer
with a step or two was that it was irregular,

the opening, a few feet
across, with floorboard edges neat

and sawn, underneath which
could be seen the topmost, leafy twigs

of a tree. I realized, or remembered
(both of which are like confirmed

science, in a dream) that this
was a clavoris: a lot like the tropical indoris

or ceiba, but higher than four hundred feet
and the color a clear blue. It

was indicated somehow, and with emphasis,
that although "Clavoris is the genus,

no individual species have ever been
identified." If, or rather, when

("if" being, in a dream, a form of motion,
already almost the past), if I lay prone

on the floor and reached
down, I could just touch

the leaves that all but brushed the nailed
under-planks. Horizontally, a mild

breeze on my hand blew across a dense
and open world. There was a sense

of fronds somewhere, bending slowly.
Far in the distance, a wedge of sea.

Through an angle
of two upper limbs, a peninsula of jungle

canopy lay out, green, tight-
laced with vines, defined as "about

two hundred feet above the jungle floor."
It closed halfway up the trunk as if around a core

—the trunk that my out-leaning glance
revealed as bigger than the circumference

of my apartment. Near the top,
a few limbs curled up

like a kind of hand,
blue-flecked, smooth. The bend

of the fingers, near my floor,
made a crow's-nest belvedere.

Anyone could jump, then, straight between
the planks, or, dangling feet-first from the planed,

hardwood edges, drop
into the cup.

From there: an easy reach out
to rows of bluish fruits;

each, I think, had a small, gray
stem. Each was heart-shaped,

about the size of a catalpa leaf, and tendril-
wrapped. My own heart was very still.

Roundabout, then: a cottonish bloom.
The tree: almost a blue foam.

I may not have seen it again,
or don't remember seeing it again.

Even so—and actually this,
I do remember now, was the premise

of the dream: any variety of the new,
the other, the adjacent, the extra-true,

any important part
of the under-world that supports

the daylit life with, evidently,
no more than a breeze, might suddenly

be glimpsed—or, from this side of dream,
guessed at or almost seen—

anywhere, angled like a shadow beneath, oh,
a lover, most likely, or straight below

another tree, or underneath something
imitating the dull, like a grating

at a crosswalk or a shelf of shoes.
What then happens are renewed

interest
and the zest

of doubt: looking at aisled crowds
of shoppers, or the separating parquet of the clouds.

EMPLOYED ON THE CLOSED WARD

Connecticut, early 1970s

Crackling and threatening, but plain
and ordinary, the world: strained

and bleak, but constrained,
sadly, by something terrible, to stay inane

and stopped. It's pre-explained
—everything—what it is, what it has to contain:

the brackish air that slowly drains,
then fills again

with voices rotten with disdain
and rage. Day after day, what can't pertain

to anything is newness or the inexplicable: purslane
in a pot that by some TV-cartoon legerdemain

balances on a skyscraper's tower vane;
or, miles underwater, on the Pacific plain,

a jellyfish longer than a commercial plane
—those are meaningless, non-germane

to the fact of being alive, that pain.
For others—you, me—outside the tight terrain:

well, recognizing the goofy or uncertain
is often what you'd most like to give them: the gain

of the loss of a main
distinction between the two groups. But the rain

(preposterous), the buildings (so self-contained),
the horizon line (floating), the stain

(spreading? why?)—whatever might get two looks on the chain
of being, has to remain

(contracting, maybe brightening again,
but unpredictably) amongst the sane.

HORIZONTAL TRAVEL

Puerto Vallarta, 1974

1.

"Oh, I must develop some less unusual desires."
Her accent—from Atlanta?—lingered on "dezaahs."

A pause. "Ah'm sure my Daddy
would just roll an' roll in his grave if he"

—another smile at me—"if he knew
what all here I've been up to."

She was maybe forty-five. There was a hot
light on the hotel pool. It was about

ten a.m. Her eyebrows, wistful
and dramatic, lifted: a signal

to her husband—thin, waiting in stillness
at another white-umbrella'd table—that this

pale, young woman in the green bikini,
who'd clambered from the deep end onto a skinny

towel, was "truly and regrettably unavailable
for now"—her mocking, sable

eyes stayed on me—"for what you
or I might call 'what-have-you's.'"

2.

Ordinary options realign in the hotel-tropics.
And what had never been a topic

of conversation or concern
becomes a repeated joke and uneasy turn

("I used to be able to think." Or, "Tammie said
you float here 'til you're dead")

in the talk among *norteamericanos*
who've stayed until the canyon—no,

the cauldron—of the fifth
or sixth week. (What would you do, if

no one could find out,
what would you try—Ecstasy? Sun Shot?

uncut heroin? Just once? *Es no
problema*, no embarrassment, and no

more danger than the amount
of danger you might secretly want.

Some special scene to watch in a special
way? The *extra especial*

—she is what? twelve? nine?—
requires only a little more time

to arrange. This is a matter
of nickels and dimes, a matter

of a certain height
achieved here upon this light

stack of pesos, *señorita, señor,*
plus a word here or there.) And your

outrage, which you supposed
would burst up—genie-style, bottle-style—purposed

and decisive, turns out
to be, like everyone's, uneasy to locate,

shifting. The grippage
of the familiar self: there's a steady slippage

as if along a wetted rope. Eventually, you really
could go mad, like anyone, here in the lobby

or under the turning fans in the tombs
of the pretty, terra-cotta rooms,

here where Old Town villas have names
but no numbers, a telegram

goes out in a day or two, milk is unpasteurized,
and the hotel pool, if you put your eyes

at water level, has a gummy crust
that's supple and mobile, like lust.

3.

I went to Mexico at twenty-six
—alone, for four weeks—to mix

with, and be more like, other people.
And "young people" do things such as "travel."

They fly to beaches for "vacations." They
don't learn beforehand the name of the oval bay

or the jagged ridge, thick with jungle,
behind the surfside palms and the tangle

of little, broken streets. They do not consult
"guidebooks" or willingly silt

themselves into the layers of a vertical,
local "history." Young people travel

within brackets, horizontally:
whatever happens where they arrive will be

the definition of the place. Bring
a passable poise or a flair for improvising.

Drink Kahlua and cream
startlingly early, eight or nine a.m.

Dine, well-dressed, alone,
at a table on the hotel's stone

lanai, the table linen-covered, elegantly wedged
into a corner with stone ledges

open to palm rattles and sea wind.
Of the strolling mariachi band,

make no requests. Order duck
or pheasant, order cold duck,

order Caesar salad (assembled before you
with silent flourishes). In the glue-

like heat next morning, probably
a young person is not seen sitting on the nubbly,

orange-glazed steps of the verandah,
watching a scorpion crawl toward something under

a raised, cracked tile. A young person
might—I wasn't sure in the flyblown

gift shop—make a purchase off the leaning rack
of oddly new paperbacks:

Agatha Christies and a collection
of plays by Oscar Wilde. And someone

young might refuse a poolside
blonde because: I wasn't certain I'd

heard her correctly
and couldn't think how to ask her, circumspectly,

to repeat herself. At dusk a one-night lover
might be taken—he was tall, from Guadalajara,

I think, pre-med—out of a vague obligation,
something to do with that earlier invitation.

4.

The invitation to La Casa del Sol
is delivered mid-morning. Out in the bowl

of the bay, the gray Pacific is still,
a synthetic metal

melted and brimming. From a parked
car above the beach, a bony, dark

Mexican in white shirt and pants, his skin
showing through extremely thin

cloth, steps with distaste, rope-sandaled,
onto the volcanic, dull-

white sand. His stiff shoulders and chest
claim something for his status,

as does the transparent outfit, worn like livery.
His hair and mustache are blurry

with oil. There's a shadow—a hard,
posturing line on the sand—when he proffers the card:

a house name, today's date (in green
ink), "nine p.m.," and a signature, "Vallarta Queen."

He does not wait to know
whether you will go.

5.

Old Town is dotted with expatriate
villas on both sides of a recurvate,

shallow river. Stone stairs, passages
between close, stone walls. Overhanging masses

of bougainvillea. A long rooftop, flat. Various
steps down from the roof to incongruous

rooms, white-stuccoed, with missing walls,
open to starlight. On ornate stands, enthralled

parrots. Greenery tubs. Espaliered
fruit on bedroom trellises. A tier

of young, mestiza women on a bench,
with ruffled dresses, fans, and entrenched

chaperones—pimps?—whose arms stay crossed
on their black-satin chests, each like a vase

standing, one at each end, for hours.
Among the twenty guests: Sugar,

a Miami LPN intent on Andrew,
a lawyer whose parasailing boat crew

almost drowned him and did not apologize
enough. "But they will." Two "merchandise guys"

from Santa Barbara—tie-dyed,
long-haired, and Ray-Ban'd—one of them snide

and too talkative, "pissed" that his partner
"dropped so many reds" during their Piper

flight that "he's been fuckin' useless
all day" to complete "the deal." Close

—deliberately?—to the rooftop edge
sits Vallarta Queen—middle-aged,

big, Bostonian, and drunk in electric-blue,
sleeveless, paisley silk, her arms at ooze

over the dark, colonial chair.
At midnight or so, when she calls you over

—"I want to meet *this* one"—
she demands your age, then

"Are you an alcoholic, too?" while silver
jewelry holds down her hands. Her eyes glaze over

at "I doubt it." They look like blue tiles.
To re-amuse herself, she pushes rolled

marijuana—like hors d'oeuvres, panached
on toothpicks in a brick of hash

at the bottom of an inlaid bowl—
towards a tall, nervous parole

officer, his blond hair buzz cut, from L.A.
The party tatters down to the bay

at about three o'clock—where somebody
you vaguely recall as somebody

you've been talking to for hours
is bobbing above his beard and under showers

of light-points in the air.
The surf is flattening. He's somber,

silent for a while before he reaches
for you. He is an apprentice

at a Sausalito mortuary. In deep baritone,
his face almost immobile, he intones,

"I feel there's going to be
a catastrophe."

6.

But in the tourist-tropics, catastrophe
is a condition of the ordinary.

Disasters that started elsewhere
branch and sprawl or are completed here.

The ice-blue water with its frost-
colored caps is always hot, and across

a month's time catastrophe
is the grounding under the flexibility

of choices, it's the repeating zero
of the balanced equation of the place. So,

if you're in the coach of an Aeronaves flight
to JFK, back to the snow of late

November, already someone else, young,
will have lurched a suitcase down the stone-rung

steps dropping from a street to the lobby
of a hotel on a beach, and already

he or she will have begun to function
among the units being factored: isolation,

shapeless time, huge heat, the flex
of *dinero,* and the peripheral, green context

that is self-sufficient. If, on the plane,
a grasshopper as long as a flashlight, pale green,

makes terrified jumps around the cabin
again and again, shockingly alone, down in

a coastal town somewhere there's Tammie,
the lithe and curling beauty

of twenty-five. Brunette, silver under the disco
strobes, notoriously from Chicago,

owner of two villas, she dances
in turn with three Indian men—their séance-

vacant faces planed and muscular—
each required to wear a cashmere sweater,

hot and white, each answering to the same
insulting name. She snaps at one of them,

"get me a drink." When an argument,
just audible from one of the faraway, front

rooms, stops, and a shot goes off,
it's predictable, standard stuff,

no one gets up from the *gringo* tables.
Amidst the waiters' gabble,

Tammie, annoyed under house lights, orders the DJ
to turn the music on again, and the spray

of her ringed hand in the smoky air
is as emphatic as her riverine Spanish. There

is, probably at the bottom of the week,
the same party invitation and the same squeak

of sandals; it might be that the exact
number of sand grains in contact

with his white cuffs, yes or no,
is all that's unpredictable. There's always also

some red-haired expatriate—sloe-eyed, tremulous,
haunted—exhaling cannabis

through the grillwork of a villa window,
disclosing to someone that twelve years ago

she arrived here on her second honeymoon.
Baffled, furious, her husband returned

stateside; she refused. She gives
no details—information here is always sieved—

but she will not joke about the floating feeling.
"Be sure you go"—and it's both reeling

and flat, her voice; it's like a censer,
the ganja smoke—"Everything is violent here."

Away from the roasted, green bubble
—leaving on a chicken-coop-topped, paint-nubbled

bus, then in a suite of fast machines
back to the confines

of a section of the northern equation,
inside which catastrophe can

add up in sequences so quick
it's like animated film—the hotel-tropics

evaporate in a kind of fizz.
A young person then carries

a longer, ambiguous list
of close calls, certain hazards narrowly missed,

due to dumb luck and accrual
of the blank disconnectedness of horizontal travel.

In the phase after that—a change
of address that probably would have arranged

itself anyway, from New England to Sausalito—
the affair with the bearded apprentice lasts, oh,

about three weeks: more units of fizz,
final fizz. Repacking, unpacking, remembering this

or that detail, some uneasiness stays,
including in dreams, for a while—several days.

Thirty to Forty

RAPHAEL

North Beach, San Francisco, 1976

At twelve, he inserted a blue hoop
in his ear. He's about forty now. It's "a loop

of sky," he tells the open-mic readers
and the besuited, bored onlookers

in the bar. The four tatterdemalion members
of his group are "Eight P.M. Poetry Room"ers.

The mic doesn't work yet. And is something
bothering him in his throat? He brings

three fingers up again to fence across his lips,
and his haggard, small mouth drops

in sometimes-audible gasps
while his thin brows lift. His hair: like a rasp,

brown; his features, gray. Maybe five feet ten.
"Presently I'm a squatter" in a boarded-up Victorian

where, he says quietly, with pride,
"Bret Harte lived for a month or two." Unemployed,

probably for years, probably on SSI;
the category: physio-mental chronic disability.

From the long-suffering and controlled
bartender (Isn't it a little old,

a poetry group in a North Beach bar
these days?), he orders water: "Large."

And takes the dignified glass back
to his corner cluster, where, off-mic,

he expounds to them about "permission":
how once, out of magazines, he cut legions

of capital letters, then tossed them down
a flight of steps in handfuls, "pounds

of them" (to what background music?),
so the skidding mix fell along a matrix

that "permitted the universe to decide,"
across each crummy step, what words it wouldn't hide

in the "Poem of the Stairs." Last week
he wrote "the rhymes for 'veins'"—he speaks

from behind the fence—"by kerosene light."
His long-sleeved shirt is thin. His wrists: white.

And outside, the self-congratulatory
streets blink and preen, with a history

that could actually be almost anywhere,
as could the chockablock buildings with their

brightly cute surfaces and standard
designs—inside some of which, tomorrow, hired

writers, as elsewhere, will assure
their minions that the art of words,

yes, is democratic, a good construction
can be put together by almost anyone

conscious or slightly attentive;
in its presence you are not in a sieve

that strains mere agony of longing
into the essence of heartbreak and non-belonging;

you aren't, no, already slotted onto a curve
by a distribution indifferent to what's deserved

by helplessness or years of hope.
"There is no originality..."—and he gropes

as if to stand, then gives up—
"in this room." He declares it again from the cup

of his metal folding chair, his starved voice rising a little,
"We have to admit that we aren't original,

and we're failed. But there *is* something else,
not as good. We must try for that something else."

And he could be the sworded archangel
if that angel had to sit, too ill

to fly to Heaven. "Mornings," he says to someone
for no clear reason, "I perform the Meditation

of Light," which he refuses to explain.
His pale eyes: tired. His jeans: stained,

baggy, the color
of the permanent *dolor*

mundi. "Dark, dark, dark,"
he chants. "Come in, dark.

I have just finished your poem"
—his skinny legs still crossed and twisted. "OM,"

he adds, which embarrasses everyone. And he stays
for a moment bent at the waist,

doubled over in a posture like prayer,
his face near his knees and just inches over

a spiral notebook, in which the blunt,
green letters, tiny, are printed from back to front.

THINGS THAT MARRY

Among the things that marry
are agendas, his and hers, along with the parry

and thrust of two wills, which, in some very
obscure, deep-water-filled-quarry

sort of way, make sense to both parties.
It's extra-discreet, how even the weaknesses marry:

counterbalanced needs not necessary
to negotiate openly ("Mary,

I need a half-acre scope for my timidity." "OK, Harry,
I need about that much for my vindictiveness.") Arbitrary

as a couple might seem (a round A with a square Z?),
if they've stayed together some ordinary

length of time, they work as a binary
unit, the two are in cahoots. Of course, what marries

also (somehow these things find each other, like rotary,
spiraling vines) are the ways in which the two then carry

out, if they reproduce, two of the primary
duties of parental life. I mean the special quandaries,

one per gender. For her: how to dare to be,
or suggest, the rebellious and contrary,

to show her children (despite the iron air she
breathes from sumptuary

rules and social atmospheres) that resistance is beautiful, sanitary,
possible and good. For him: how to be the adversary

against a library
of threats from maternal avidity, how to be wary

of a loved woman on a child's behalf, an intercalary.
(It's enough to make you wonder where He and She

find the wherewithal to carry
it all past the starting point. Being unaware clearly

is a help—that chary
refusal to remember much about any of this for very

long.) What also marries,
of course, are strengths, or halves thereof: bare, de-

crepit traits and sturdy, sweet ones—cherries
with lemons—that first linked up during those harried,

early years when our parents' personalities
reproduced in us, in bits, the recombinatories

of self, shaggy and lush and something like (though only
sort of, something like) the TT's

and Tt's and tt's and tT's
of lone Brother Mendel's orderly peas.

THIS ONE

To J.

How did it happen, this
unlikeliness?

An emphasis
in your past, was it, or mine, so a crisis

was step-asideable? What criss-
crossed, considering the rigor mortis

of my adolescence and the non-bliss
of yours, followed by labored learning's slow osmosis

for two decades after that? The x-axis
dots somehow met the axis

of y, with the current bright result. And I know this
much: it's all "huh?" and "whatsis?"

to me. You say you dunno, either. Genesis,
meanwhile, is

all that anyone longs to know about: the first basis
of the body, of those parents over there, of this

sphere in space, or anything that is
changing, such as, oh, the Coriolis

effect on the breeze, or a shift in stasis
so feeling can begin, including this

one, emphatic as clematis
rickracking now across the backyard trellis.

A quick crushing: is
that what the facts are doing—re-synthesis

in a micromoment as the past compresses
into the one fat dot of "This Is

It"? So a back-of-the-neck kiss
and a bronze recovered below the Acropolis

connect instantly to the Lewis
and Clark expedition, the total Kiwanis

membership, and a recipe with orris?
Eventually, since my secret name was Limnanthis

(in my twenties) and since you like waffles, is
it certain we'd happen, without work or promises?

THE MOST ORDINARY THING IN THE WORLD:
RUBENS' "PORTRAIT OF ISABELLA BRANDT"

The Cleveland Museum of Art

To her left, three times her size,
another seventeenth-century woman, ablaze

in red, with tiara and gold buttons
—and in possession of an adoring son

who is not so much as glanced at—
celebrates the satin rarity and isolate

privilege that attend certain
chilly arrangements of money and women.

The Isabella portrait is a head
and torso on a background of mud-

gray smudge. Her black-velvet dress,
high-collared, edged with simple lace,

respectfully props her bosom
and face as if she were a soft variety of gem.

Her head lifts well above
the gown, independent of constraint or of

the chaos behind her, which nevertheless
has almost dissolved a few of her flying wisps

of hair. She has turned—with a slight
assertion?—a little to her right,

while her almond-shaped and hazel
eyes, large, under arched, quizzical

brows, gaze steadily out
with a look so saucy, so out-and-out

amused and confident
and wily and tolerant,

it has to be the proliferative
look of a wife,

one embedded in what is at times
the most ordinary thing in the world, a kind of chime:

the love of a full-grown woman
for the full-grown man

who loves her. Which she knows,
of course, and knows that he knows

she knows. A gold clasp, as if required,
is in her pulled-back, casual, chestnut hair;

at her ear a pearl, not accentuated;
a necklace also is perfunctorily suggested

against the treasure of her open skin. No ring or
glove competes with her right-hand fingers

and their ept salute as they encircle
one breast and press its velvet-hidden nipple.

The painter, like any wise husband, does not argue
with the wryness of Eve. He gives her her due,

admitting that she understands,
completely, the welcomed man before her, and

that the beautiful, small lips,
pressed together firmly above the chip

of her dimpled chin,
are about to flare into a laugh at him.

* * * * *

But the completion date says 1625,
and the subject is known to have died

the following year, at thirty-five. She has tried
with her turn to hide it, but her right eye

is slightly heavy-lidded?, and the skin
at her immaculate temples is thin,

as if long tugged-at by something more
stubborn than fatigue. The recorder

in his record has not tried to pretend
that the black fabric that extends

to surround her is not the final
blackness of a shroud, nor that she's not a partial

figure, in a dress
that falls away into nothingness.

He knows, of course, and knows
that she knows he knows.

Strokes of shadow, minutely thin
at the top of her throat, are as if he were cupping her chin.

* * * * *

Which is why, at night,
when ghosts of other masters of light

and line stroll in groups through these numbered
rooms—the perfecters of ambered

battlefield and dragon braveries,
portrayers of soft or atrocious pieties,

of the world with its darkness and loads
and vegetation along buttery roads

and convivialities of the given norms,
including commerce as a form

of optimism—it is this gallery they step into last.
They've sauntered past

marble dadoes and taupe walls
and multiple dozens of hanging panels,

or paused on the parquet to continue
old arguments and reconstrue:

"Thank God, there's no Vermeer!
(from a distant room): Nine colors,

his miserable palette! Would a tenth
have broken him?" Elsewhere, Van Goyen

to some member of the Fauves:
"What tells the time of day, mon brave,

is the humidity! Look at the Cuyp or
Ruisdael! Or the Steen! Moisture

is an adhesive, it constricts
the light around the edges of the object!"

A quiet voice—Campin to Bouts?: *"That green*
on the cape: how many layers? Fourteen?

Twelve?" And Delacroix: *"Has he told anyone?"*
Meaning, has the Antwerpian

revealed the details of his invention,
those buried charcoal stripes, diagonal, uneven,

by which he's made the illusion
of skin: not with an application

of dark colors onto gessoed ground,
but the reverse, like life itself, laying down

pale colors onto scumbled dark.
About which there's no argument in this vertical park:

flesh, the vehicle of emotional commerce,
by anyone else

is approximation
and bluff. This is their station,

then, Isabella's room, at the brink
of morning. Shouldering in, then linked,

some with arms akimbo,
they assemble in rows

like burghermeisters or civic guards,
and they regard

this two-foot, wood-framed portrait.
Whether, this time, they look at

the frizz of curls so resolutely freed
beside her ear; or notice instead

that the viewer is allowed to take the painter's place,
his mortal place, to receive this woman's gaze;

or whether they study the peaches of paint
so thinly applied to darkness, they squint and nod, silent.

ONCE UPON

Cass, West Virginia

My friends' children, six and four,
played in picnic grass with their father.

Katherine—belle-lettrist, editor,
who once defined a "child" as "another

chance to fall in love"—seated between roots
below a red maple, mused:

"What can we tell them, at their age? We don't
believe religious doctrines, but if we don't

tell them 'God' exists and knows
what they're up to, how

will they behave when we're not with them,
in the room?"

Your new girl and boy—well: tell them about,
oh, the bushiness and twigs. How,

once upon a time including now,
there was and is the wide, high Kapow

Bush of the World. On it the busy,
different twigs are wiggling prettily,

each with its own style, but twig-
connected by Time, which is a big

stem, down to roots of metal and water.
(Add something about light.) Here, on an outer

branch, are lots of double-legs with nerve-
balls, large, tucked into curved

heads. The Kapow has need of those brains
to fix some problems on the shared terrain

and help out everything. Inform your twigs
that his and her encephalons are rigged

just beautifully and will be perfect for the job.
They'll share the thinking-work for blobs

of alligator eggs, the focused rose,
the curious trees, the pensive tomatoes;

they'll be the thinking rain, the thinking asteroid,
the thinking ice, the thinking void.

Of course, there's a different story
for anyone visiting the parental library.

In This Very Room (category: suspense)
makes clear it makes little difference

what any parent overtly abjures,
threatens, pleads or hortatores,

because a child—"X"—can never occupy
a room not already occupied

by X's early images of Dad's and Mom's
real attitudes. Including later, adult rooms,

where X won't fail to consult again his lengthy
toddler-records, *The Book of M. and D.,*

in which his parents' factualities
—sweetness, selfishness, hypocrisies—

were recorded with submillimeter accuracy
via the tones and hesitations of adult bodies,

detected by X despite protests to the contrary
or punishments of the contrary.

What X does later—ethical, unethical—
will be a photograph of what always was the real

information. Katherine, introspective, dear
and long-time friend, let me dog-ear

this page in this scary story
to issue a thank-you to those hoary,

gruesome progenitors of yours
—up-class and low-heart, both of them—for

providing such negative examples
in knife-like silhouette. They must have had ample

wishes (somewhere, tightly boxed) for goodness,
for distance from heart-crudity and rudeness,

wishes that elaborated you (who'd play fair
with Hamlin's Pied Piper

and thereby save the mountain town).
They both receive this afternoon's

Oh-Well Award, though it was cruel
in their Grubby Kingdom, what with their renewal

every day of *Me! Doing What I Please!*
(issued in underground editions as

The Basilisk Factory of Tears),
which they reviewed, I suppose, every grim few hours

—that one lying page—for its yellow claims
that now, as once upon a time,

children do not notice a gabble
of motives, and parents are safely invisible.

Forty to Fifty

BRIGHT THING ACROSS A BRIGHT TABLE

To J.

Lately you've felt the weight, I think,
of superfluousness; at the brink

of late middle age felt the drub
of extraneousness like a club

in the night against your heart.
A fine daughter and grandson cart

away, this very minute,
part of your body into the future, and yet

the body of your hopes stays a little
bruised. The percentile ranking, meanwhile,

of your Life Accomplishment Quotient
gleams so golden and so argent,

there are probably few your uneasy
state could be confided to and be seriously

believed. Look at you. Thing of unstable
and stable matter. Bright thing across a bright table.

Only the first two vacuums,
false and true, those fat, tiny rooms

that were the early Universe,
amounted to Necessity: unsuperfluous,

unique, relentlessly meaningful.
Since then nothing has been really full

or thoroughly significant.
Much more about which, though, I can't

tell you, being material
myself. However, if they were tracked, your serial

trajectories—the steady blaze
of infrared, say, or electron rays

emanating off the assorted quarks of you
as if from a sparking, still-new

dynamo—well, I'd have to accessorize
with special spectacles while your blue eyes

fraternize with nova swirls
and star-jets and emission shells,

luminosities micro- and stupendous,
each non-vacuumlike and therefore, yes, gratuitous,

in no way unlike yourself: of necessity
just beaming and gorgeous. Love me?

ORDINARY ILLNESS

About mortal illness in its chronic,
slow modes, there's a—well, not metronomic,

but steady revision of outlook.
Right away you get impatient with the look

and behavior of flowers,
all those seen-before colors

and habits of being.
Live a year and novelty becomes a thing

that's ultimate, a sort
of buried treasure and you the pirate

with an incomplete map: the rare
is where?—out the window, upstairs,

beyond the usual inclinations.
A doubloon is the chunk of information

you didn't know before. Live two years
and the time you keep spending in the Cancer

Lounge, with its clichéd music
and croupier—his obvious, sleek

outfit and skinny fingers—is no longer
so interesting, but you linger

with relish over, of all things, neutrality,
good-old, even-steven impartiality,

because it can feel, compared to your
fervid human investments, more

simple, fresh, and mysterious. Live four years
(after your first, held-breath wager,

which had to do with the odds
of reaching year three), and the rodomontade

of solemnities the world pronounces
about what is, after all, a few ounces

of cell division gone maximally dull
—all the beige brochures and sentimental

portrayals—well, they seem like a balance,
on ironic days, for everyone's well-meaning silence

on other aspects of the topic,
including the illness-logic

of a constant paradox:
that your situation makes a Difference, locks

everything about you into the Frightful-
Magical, but also makes no difference at all.

Live six years and the sudden
recurrence of dread now and then

becomes something interesting
in itself—not remote, but interesting

to look at, because the null
of dread takes place, if it's going to, during travel,

when the setting is beautiful
and the wide display has some detail

that reminds you of the green-baize betting rooms
—with their limited novelty, including doom.

UFIs

Not a terrible day
exactly, just a longish, afternoon foray

into Frustrate Land, with the usual souvenirs:
compression, hurt, some disarray. But in the near

distance, over the mall's parking lot, crowds
are ambling now the way fish know how

to amble, and clouds in the east, thin and dusky,
frond up over the lighted movie marquee

under which a couple of friends already wait,
both expert at opening the gate

to the Land of OK. Still,
it's from somewhere else, the sudden feel

of lift, it's like an inner flare
after a breath of something like an off-Earth air,

and abruptly all the molecules
in your medium-sized, organic module

find themselves well across the border
into the Land of Fine, re-intact and in good order.

Oh, I wouldn't claim it isn't routine,
just an epi-event: a burst, maybe, of dopamine

after a protein dinner; or ATP charging
across membranes F and R, thereby enlarging

a lot of peace-of-mind receptors.
Still, it's the kind of thing you could register

—being such a specific experience—
on a life-list of emotional events:

the giant and moderate loves, graduation
out of loss or into loss, this or that occasion

of motherhood or fatherhood,
repetitions of bad and good

varieties of heartfelt self-defense,
plus about a hundred and seventeen instances

of Unidentified Flying Integrationals,
each independent of the will,

arriving out of nowhere and good, maybe, for hours,
who knows? Who knows a thing about the ordinary powers?

FOR THE SOMEWHAT EXPERIENCED

*And in defense of Emma Bovary's husband,
boorish, benighted, sexually inept, who died
of an obsessed, possibly perfect love*

There is a thicketed nest
of questions that can't be quieted or guessed

without the odd, relentless facts
delivered by bodies in the act

of inquiry. Common flesh
can take you, occasionally, into a fresh

stillness only the solitudes of intimacy can invest
into you, or remove. The exultant best,

the long-gripped illusions, reverse-discoveries,
humiliating loss, mess, maybe

also certain bleak totalities pressed
into fear and anguish: accept nothing less.

Then, Now,
Here and There

LEAVES

Brownish-gray, difficult to see
in the forest understory

bordering the savannahs, a cat-sized mammal
—furred, fetching, primate, nocturnal—

continues to have small
increases in its life expectancy and better survival

of its nested litters by not being able to see very well.
None of its offspring finds itself with a special

advantage if, nimble
like the others, it also has unusual

vision—extending, say, into infrared potentials
that might discriminate far beyond the frontal

foliage, or having the retinal
packing and exquisitely knotted neural

connections that long ago made for the chromal
powers of birds. Listening from an aerial

V in the branches, warning with forepaw signals
and shrieks, it's a raucous animal

whose overall
needs happen not to include a use for fine tonal-

contrast distinction—though that might have revealed,
as if sprayed on a curved wall,

stars shining in daytime through the scrawl
of the moving air. A few millennia of additional

shapings and preferential
events, and it's larger, ninety pounds, non-arboreal,

with just enough perceptual
apparatus that it can detect (in a gradual

way and only in the fall
of what it will later call

a "year" in the "natural
world") some of the emphatic, feral

colors broadcasting from varietals
of leaves and grass throughout the vegetal

universe—color tones that, in the retinal
cones of this animal,

stay mostly inaccessible,
barricaded for three seasons by the greens of chlorophyll.

Overhauled
some millennia later, still with original

sensory equipment but now less tailed,
more lightly furred, bipedal

and bulgingly cortical,
the more or less same animal,

having figured out some advantages in detecting the invisible,
paws with technical

tools opening farther into the real,
while guessing that any wherewithal

throughout the cosmos might be also non-autumnal:
that we might not—or not yet?—be able

to see
either the old forest or the new trees.

A WALL OF ICE

Late Pleistocene, North America,
ca. 11,000 B.P.

There might be a moment
when a thing becomes un-ordinary, bent

—suddenly?—away from the commonplace.
Was it, for the mounting edge of ice

on the Laurentide sheet, when infinitesimal
bricks, each a crystal

mortared with cold, reached the level
of fifty feet? Or was it later, when the mantle

under the Midwest had sagged below
a slab-weight of boulders in snow

and the same ice wall, sheer-fronted,
stood two and a half miles high—blunt-

topped but sloping gradually
westward from its three-

mile height at Hudson Bay? Sunlight
at every dawn shot a straight

line across a continuous cliff
from Greenland west to the midriff

of the continent. Major rivers south
of Canada ran northward then, without

much incident, for hundreds of miles. But
a moment would arrive, or a set

of moments?, when the rivers' gray
and white chutes, in a piled-up melee

—rolling down the side
of the Appalachian plateau as if on a slide—

struck full force into the solid ice and,
with nowhere to turn, had to bend

beneath themselves, churning up gravel
and mud with currents that dug like sandhog shovels.

Forested terrain for hundreds of miles rumbled
like a factory floor while the rivers stumbled

deeper, to six hundred feet down
at some places—self-confluencing, to drown

without a trace, self-poured
into what would be the steep-shored

buckets of five inland lakes. But
those moments were so many, it might

still have been ordinary, the smash
of waters climbing as a splash

against the lower wall to half a mile high, un-
changing, for forty centuries. There was high, un-

wavering fog; day and night,
the same pitch to the roar and the same slight

Doppler shift—registered by a deer,
white-tailed, sprinting from a gray wolf near

the shore, crouched under aspen and everyday
pines. White and gray

mornings on the growing lakes were followed by
white and gray afternoons, every

moment of which several paralyzed
rainbows arched above icebergs the size

of small towns. No doubt
even the guano quantity stayed about

the same on the slow-bobbing
iceberg chunks, where the mobbing

grebes and mergansers flew out
to fish for the fry of pike and trout,

alongside gulls by the thousands. Geese
kept scouting the ice-filigreed weeds

amidst beaver, otter, mice—species too numerous
to be remarkable but not over-numerous

for briefly enough to be remarkable,
either. The gulls' cries, already stable

for forty million years before the Pleistocene,
were not more soft or raucous than

if their glacial cliff had been
a ledge of just ten

inches—the same gull species patrolling now
in short swoops or shouting in crowds

every afternoon
from the piers on Lake Michigan,

in the usual haze: commonplace, sort of, in a way,
in their as-yet-unchanged white and gray.

HISTORY OF AN ORDINARY DOUBT

1.

In southern Mesopotamia,
around two and a half millennia

B.C., the expanding city of Mashkan-shapir
committed itself to a new manufacture:

synthetic basalt slabs, for miles of tall
and vastly thick exterior walls. Metallurgical

and fine ceramic techniques were somehow
combined; it's not known how.

Riverborne local silt
is what the blocks resemble, if that silt

had been furnaced, melted, then forced
to cool so slowly—across

a monitored interval
of thirty or forty hours—that crystals,

black, a proto-basalt, would precipitate.
Change your building and you change your fate,

of course, including the fate of a notion
that would stand for five more centuries, in stone...

2.

Quick money in the form of barley,
in bagged equivalents of silver. Saved money,

hidden in chests, was usually silver coils
the shape and size of Slinkys. Oils

of sesame, flax, olive, mustard.
Busy boat-roads; written records; a high living standard.

Vaulted granaries, baths; pillared halls. Specialized
occupations under minutely organized,

continuing governments. Pomp, wide prosperity,
ease for hundreds of years. Black-line geometry

on red-slip pots. Flutes, theater. Lebanon
trees in groves, mostly cedar. Citrus, watermelon,

horses, zebu, elephants, pigs, chickens.
Civic complexes, the first to be reckoned

accurately, with guardian walls
forty feet thick and as tall

as the mid-level stars—walls resting on
a single platform of bricks, a foundation

shared by all the city. Elaborate glass,
electrum, turquoise, gold. A middle-class

timber merchant, chatting with his daughter
in Mohenjo-daro, reclines in clear water

rushing through ceramic pipes
to his third-floor bath. More pipes

lie under the world's first straight streets.
Far off, the great pyramids are recently complete.

Ziggurats are half a thousand years in the future; three-
quarters of a thousand years to Hammurabi.

Dark smoke in praise of the city, the God,
circling upward,

obscures the citadel on the hottest days,
the brick citadel whose enormous vaults are raised

on a base that alone rises fifty feet
above the streets—above the sweeps

of awning cloths shadowing the alleys
layer upon layer, sloping across the passageways

so that light from the Sun God, not so intense,
is like a thin application of the lightest of unguents.

3.

Stranger, you would have to be beguiled
on Harappan beer, you would have to be a child,

mad as a monkey or one of the prodded bulls,
you would have to be fearful

as our foolish ancestors, who trembled
at the thought there might not be a god

to succor them; you would have to be all
these follies to doubt the real

presence of our Protector. Where
is the Lord of the Sun? Look here

at these walls, hardened in the gaze
of the God, who long ago revealed the way

to make this living thing, the city,
disclosed it to our priests in auguries

and dreams. This is the God's high body
around us, gift from the God, what He

made for us out of power and timelessness.
Settlements of peoples long before us

and the towns of great Egypt now
have no walls. The lesser gods move them about

at will, like dunes of sand. It is at Mashkan-Shapir
and Babylon, at Sippar and Sumer

and Susa that the proper relation
of God is displayed to the stations of man.

As a child, my father's father knew these faienced walls,
which were already old. You look at the eternal

here. Children of my children's children will
hang new faience to praise these walls.

4.

It would have taken more than
a decade, probably almost a generation

amidst the ruin, before anyone
still alive after the first disintegration

would have realized
—while the distant, rotted city at sunrise

looked sometimes like fractured bone
and grief hardened under the sun—

that what had been known
with certainty was gone

and could not return; rebuilding
would not be possible. In huddling,

drying settlements, to men and women
in new solitudes, an old fear returned,

re-entered the human mind
as a permanent marauder, and worse than flame or wind.

THE WORLD IN FRONT OF YOU

Shadows of clouds run away from the sun,
dark and fast across the ground. None

escapes. The great hawk circles above
the great vole and the dive

of the hawk is the edge of a knife.
Under the claw, the vole's life

fights on in front of the red gate,
then gives its spirit, bright

and quick, to the hawk and the strong,
new young of the hawk. Everything

must die in struggle and pain
or it does not die well. By these signs

we know how to be whole,
how to be sacred. The vole

dies held against a rock.
We also will strike upon a slab of rock,

catching the bounty in strong, brown bowls,
first the blood from the great vole's

talisman, our king, then blood
from our strongest captives. In patient crowds,

we will test them, one by one,
under the hawk, on altars close to the sun.

There will be terror, piety,
shrieks, the proper order, blood to the knees,

honor of flesh flayed into tassels.
We will record on clay vessels

the howling mouths of our enemies,
who stay our brothers and our necessity,

worthy of song, worthy of memory.
What is, is what must be,

for the great world does not conceal
or lie. What is before you is real.

AÏ KHANOUM

*"Justice Freedom Democracy Knowledge
Experience Happiness"—on the lintel of a 1930s
brick-and-sandstone building on the Ohio State
campus. "It looks," a friend said, "as if it were
trying to talk."*

Supertalls across the world
reach half a mile high, or almost, but look furled,

uneasy, closed—a little abject?
None has a grade-level plaque on the subject,

confidently incised, of what makes
for a well-lived human life: what that would take,

and in what sequence. But in
Delphos, repeated for centuries by the Python

and carved into marble bases throughout the realm
of Hellenes—even in Aï Khanoum

in Bactria, cut into its mud-brick blocks
five thousand miles from the land-locked

oracle—is the summary of difficulties, in stages,
that allow for greatness at any age

in the lives of Greeks: "As a child, be well-
behaved. In your youth, self-controlled.

Through your middle years, be just. Later,
also, a reliable advisor.

At the end of life" (Does the list somehow tell us
how? Is it like reaching a white-beach terminus

of an archipelago?),
"be free of sorrow."

Fifty to Sixty

A RESTLESSNESS

*Based loosely on a sonnet
by Gérard de Nerval*

If I could speak to all humanity,
I'd have a question: how could we be,

even with our sprays of thought,
the only owners, world-throughout,

of authority and subtlety,
here where vitality

is exploding, blowing
out from the centers of everything?

Some of the forces we've seized
—the more minor powers of water, sun, breeze—

are administered, yes, at our will
under certain conditions, but all the while,

when you or I or anyone
looks down this long table, there, turned

at an angle, is the chair
marked "Universe," its other living contents elsewhere.

What we, at times, suspect:
we'd be intelligent—more—if we'd respect

a restlessness hidden in other beasts.
Parrots subtract and add to at least

the number six; the closed eyes of birds
flicker during sleep in the figured

middle of some sort of dreams. Butterflies achieve
the learning of more colors. Crocodiles grieve

now and then. In the Bering Strait,
a humpback interrupts his song, migrates

to Patagonia, returns as long
as twelve months later and takes up that song

at the note where he left off.
A moss and an oak are two of the soft

or rigid shapes
an invisible energy takes, and what it drapes

is emphatic nakedness. The almost-floral
structure of minerals and metals

is more of that power, burgeoning
with potentials, with something

that might or might not love. Objects
change, they're more or less circumspect,

more or less sensate, their forces
latent but near at hand. Down the course

of this room, these blind, "solid" walls
—mahoganied, evolving—watch us all

in their way, and on the vibrating lattices
of their smallest interstices

the capacity for huge movement is attached
—no doubt too long attached

to what's been our destructive
use for it. Be careful: while we live,

we will not know what unimposing,
ordinary thing

is slowly becoming a zone
concentered on a tiny, but to-be-fully-grown

identity. In the way a complex
eye is born—tightly covered by a convex

lid—like that, a purity exists.
It moves, it swells a little, grows restless;

restrained again, it almost groans.
It longs to look out, even through the crust of stones.

JOHANNES BRAHMS

(Webern, Carter, early Mahler,
Dvořák, Williams, Elgar...)

Near the end, he burned trunks of letters:
his publishers,' Clara Schumann's, his mother's.

Work not better than good, not perfect in every bar,
had already fed the cast-iron doors

of his apartment stoves for forty years.
Uncouth, graceless, he couldn't easily bear

the lumbering unruliness
and clamor of everydayness

—all insufficiently composed.
Daily for decades, with anguish, he'd know

he was unfit for the married order
he longed for, given his teenage stint in bars

at the Hamburg brothel-docks, where
he'd rescued his impecunious father

and acquiescent, greedy mother
by pounding jig tunes for half-dressed whores.

That he was dandled and teased there, used
for his pretty face and long hair and blue,

cornflower eyes; that he was drunk at thirteen,
fourteen, lurching home at dawn with migraine,

tutored in the noisome, sewer self;
that women for the rest of his life

would be dream-vessels of transformation,
idealized but distrusted, used for inspiration,

then abandoned: all that made him curt,
of course, and brash, peasant-crude, alert

to any chance to bluster an advantage,
loud, lonely, savage

—with overcoat pockets full of sweets
for urchin children begging in the street.

(Ives, Sibelius, Berg, Busoni,
Schoenberg, Stravinsky...)

That he snarled as often as he blushed
(in old age even more easily), given to rushes

of open tears—those, too, were the family romance
at work, dreadful, but in circumstances

that mean little now. Late in life, though,
that he was sure his work would vanish with no

offspring, thousands of hours in solitary rooms
for music soon to be forgotten, doomed

with the last fling of rich Vienna's bourgeoisie;
that he agonized, certain of his triviality

—well, there's a seizure of protest, you rustle in the auditorium
of the mind; you try, ridiculously, to call to him,

and it's maddening, where's the list
(not Bruckner, not Wagner, not the sneering Liszt...)

of the next century's consoling names, none
of whom, without him, could have grown

as new, as dense, as startling or essential? It's some odd
opening you want, to drag him out of his time. But the god

of the ordinary, brother of Rhadamanthus,
insists all consolation must

stay within the confines of the life, tone-deaf
(Nielsen, Bartok, Prokofieff...)

to the future's calling and calling of
his name; impervious to extra love.

What you can wish for?—is the usual,
the likely, the probable.

Across the Elizabeth Bridge, say, in 1886,
away from the big-bottomed kitsch

of the Ringstrasse, when he'd stomp steadily north
to Prater Park—pince-nez on a cord

across his bulging waistcoat, a bowler hat,
one round hand cocked behind the back

of a gray, worn topcoat—he would not be hard
to recognize, tramping the four-mile park

any autumn day for a quarter century. Great-
bearded; trousers higher than his boots; short,

square, and block-faced; a wide-browed
owl with azure eyes, his memory now

at fifty-three still comparable to Mozart's.
More thoroughly than anyone alive, he knows thought

and feeling are identical, the most accurate
portrait of misery is found in a waltz, that

ugliness cantilevers through the decent
as well as the beautiful and is placed in their present

service, that attempts
to live inside illusions are more unkempt

and spiritually stunting than to live without them, all.
So, from the category of the Non-unusual:

near the merry-go-round, amusement end of the Park,
trolling eastward in the early dark,

a pretty grisette—professionally fond
of the good-natured Herr Doktor, so blond

and generous—spies him under the lindens,
on a bench, the famous tears on his cheeks, his chin

deep-lowered into his beard, cigar ash
on his knuckles, right boot tapping the grass.

Probable: she'd twirl an orange-flounced parasol
and, in bright pink silk, she'd sashay as she calls

his name—curving like a bridge as she leans
toward him. Her fingernails, let's say, are unusually clean.

Likely: she'd reach out a yellow, mitaine'd glove to cup
his chin and lift it, level with the distant Danube, up.

ORDINARY STASIS

> *"The more one looks closely at those who
> apparently were the most active participants
> during the Terror, the more one discovers in them
> something passive and mechanical."* Joseph de
> Maistre

Evil—this is not news—is a form
of conservatism. What its norm,

hourly, keeps
in place is not empowerment but deep,

self-hidden, secretly pathetic
lack of power, in a position static,

stuck. Whether brutality to a child
or a moment's condescension from the high-heeled

and arch-browed; whether a heaped murder
of millions or a blurred,

niggling meanness; whether raving or sane,
displayed in methods inane

or new, evil's origin is not mysterious,
and, also secretly, we do know this.

It's among us not from promptings in a garden
by a talking snake, but as repetition

of contempt and viciousness in the early lives
of the hurt people who raised us, who didn't realize

—or, in despair, could not care about—
the parental past they, too, were replicating. It's an in-to-out

mechanicalness: our learned-
from-them self-loathing and needy panic, burned

in, rigid in the mind, and that long-ago
parent—cold, hapless, unknowing, lonely—oh,

must be brought back, might be kept near
by being perfectly imitated. And the trigger?,

the noticed helplessness of someone
else on whom to be revenged—even your own

loved child. The neutral Now
becomes the terrible Then. Probably the how

and when of change are what's individual,
brave, and unidentified. In the killer, meanwhile,

in me, in you, evil
is the over-obedient thing, over-traditional,

tormented, robotic, linked to its own far past
and a past and a past

as another in a series of cut-paper dolls.
It's the stasis of man that is the Fall.

M. CH. LABITTE

Three Indian women, in jeans,
elegantly young, triangularly arranged

in the coffeehouse easy chairs, gesticulate
and laugh, watching themselves be great-

of-future, modern—but not
watching themselves be vulnerable. Spots

of blond tables behind them
in the yellow room are rimmed

with high-school students: two teenage girls,
six boys. Backpacks at their feet, they curl

forward, frowning at their phones and tablets.
Black geometries in the gray carpet

fly from the bustling, far counter
toward me in this windowed corner

—middleaged, red-scarf'd, red-jeaned,
like a large and long-lived tropical bird. Between

the lemon wall and my paper cup:
a small book, seven by five, a strip

of black tape down the spine, pages
yellowed, edited in the Napoleonic age

by a man who assumed two abbreviations
and no listed affiliation

would stay enough to identify himself. He pleads
in a seemly French, M. Ch. Labitte,

that we reconsider the verse by a certain
dramatist and hortatory Jacobin,

his older near-contemporary
who did not do all he might have—possibly—

to rescue, in Paris, his gifted brother from
the blood-addicted mob. The pantomime,

brief and supplicating, the past
performs for every future is fast-

performed now for me, to whom it falls
to assess both sets of their decisions. Unimaginable

me: with my horseless vehicle
steered through lanes of moving metal,

"lights" and wires inserted everywhere,
a machine overhead heavier than air,

these "acrylic" surfaces, this label on
the little book ("inter-library loan")—

all weird unto distortion,
not unlike, probably, the proportions

of my love-arrangements
and decades of choices, including moments

in "voting booths;" including, too,
the erstwhile cultural authorities I do

not acknowledge, scarcely even remember
the outlines of. ("Mam'selle?" "Monsieur

Labitte? Bonjour.") His surprise no doubt
would include some gratitude with an ort

or two of reasonable resentment.
November light outside, on the circumference

of the depopulated patio, glitters
on steel railings; the window near

my right extends a yellow stretch
toward leafless trees—sycamore, beech—

down the suburban street.
How long will there be ground-based streets

or familiar trees? And what might a self
in the Unimaginable Future, the U. F.,

select as weight from the lives in this room?
Anything? The past with its upturned palms

requests the benefit—amidst the blur—
of the doubt, asks everyone to remember

we all send a brother
to the guillotine in one way or another

—as will you, O future friend—
that our lives stay made of the maudlin,

the mediocre, and something that deserves
to be translated and conserved,

like the seven-line section
from this edition's

total pages of a hundred and a half.
No doubt, *Monsieur* or *Mam'selle* U. F.,

if you live you know that—you, hunting
for fresh company, for surprise, for things

with antique oddity? For crossing the blurry
regions to this detail of the past, *merci.*

And *bonne chance*: how odd and frail
may be your future too, you whose good will

and sagesse and alien wit
might be resented, a little, if we knew of it.

NOTES

The Clavoris

The tropical *Ceiba pentandra* (the silk-cotton, or kapok tree) has reportedly reached heights of more than three hundred feet. "Indoris" is an invention.

Employed on the Closed Ward

The deep-sea Praya, a gelatinous, colonial animal with multiple stomachs, has been measured at one hundred thirty feet, longer than a blue whale or commercial airliner.

Things That Marry

From cross-breeding pea plants in his monastery garden, Gregor Mendel (1822-1884) identified the genetic Law of Separation: units of heredity exist in pairs that separate, then rejoin in new combinations during reproduction. For the trait of tallness (T) or shortness (t), he inferred the distribution pattern of TT, tt, tT and Tt.

The Most Ordinary Thing in the World:
Rubens' "Portrait of Isabella Brandt"

Isabella's portrait is in the Reinberger Gallery, alongside Anthony van Dyck's "Portrait of a Woman and Child."

Delacroix, Renoir, and any number of students of painting have tried to duplicate the application of flesh tones onto a dark background, a technique Rubens developed around 1614. To date, no one has succeeded.

Once Upon

See Alice Miller, *Banished Knowledge: Facing Childhood Injuries*, Rev. ed., translated by Leila Vennewitz (New York: Anchor Books, 1991).

Bright Thing Across a Bright Table

In most inflationary-theory accounts of the universe, the near-vacuum of present space was preceded by a colossally energized "false vacuum" of dark energy that destabilized and expanded before the Big Bang. It was during the transition from one vacuum to another that the basic properties of matter were set.

Leaves

When autumn dryness breaks down the chlorophyll in plants, some of the reds, purples and golds constantly reflected from foliage (and visible to many other animals) are more detectable by the current human eye.

A Wall of Ice

With the retreat of the glaciers and rebounding uplift of the North American continent—which now tilts southward—no major river in the U.S. empties to the north.

History of an Ordinary Doubt

The first walled cities, beginning ca. 2800 B.C. in the Indus Valley and Mesopotamia, provided a new protection that almost certainly would have been associated with the favor of a god. Physical encirclements (the walls of Babylon were so wide, six chariots could be driven side by side around the flat top) ushered in a period of unprecedented stability and prosperity lasting for five centuries. Until ca. 2300 B.C., throughout the Fertile Crescent, no fully organized national state had ever disintegrated.

The World in Front of You

Belief in animal emblems, part of the essentialist outlook common to most early cultures, assumes that nature's overt appearances are completely truthful and the surface of an object reliably expresses its inner essence.

Aï Khanoum

Founded as Eucratidia, Aï Khanoum was an affluent oasis city colonized by Hellenes after the conquest of Bactria by Alexander the Great in 329 B.C. Its location now in northern Afghanistan is close to the India border.

A Restlessness

See "Vers dorés," by Gérard de Nerval.

Johannes Brahms

See Jan Swafford, *Johannes Brahms: A Biography* (New York: Alfred A. Knopf, 1997).

Ordinary Stasis

See Joseph de Maistre, *Considérations sur la France, 1796* (Paris: Editions Complexe, 1999).

See also Alice Miller, *The Drama of the Gifted Child,* Rev. ed., translated by Ruth Ward (New York: Basic Books, 1997).

M. Ch. Labitte

Marie-Joseph Blaise de Chénier (1764-1811), the younger brother of André and a didactic playwright, poet and pamphleteer, was one of the few prominent Jacobin revolutionaries who lived to prosper as a bureaucrat under Napoleon, possibly because of a talent for the quisling. He lived to hear the accusation that neither he nor his father had done all that was possible to rescue his brother from the guillotine. Lines 8-14 of his "Discours sur la Raison," *Poésies de Marie-Joseph Blaise de Chénier,* ed. M. Ch. Labitte (Paris: Charpentier, Libraire-Éditeur, 1844), translated by Diane Furtney:

It makes good sense to acknowledge
that Reason accomplishes everything—in knowledge,

talent, genius, the verve of spirit,
certainly also taste and virtue. What is it,

virtue, but Reason put into practice
firmly? Talent? It's

Reason with a bit
of éclat.

Exquisitely expressed,
Reason takes the form of confidence and zest.

Good taste means delicate
good sense—again, Reason—while genius, that

of any place or time,
is Reason raised to the sublime.

ACKNOWLEDGMENTS

Grateful acknowledgment is made to the journals in which these poems appeared, often in earlier versions:

Bellingham Review: "The Clavoris"
Chiron Review: "The Most Ordinary Thing in the World: Rubens' 'Portrait of Isabella Brandt'"
The Cream City Review: "A Restlessness"
Critical Quarterly (England): "History of an Ordinary Doubt," "Leaves," "Raphael"
TheDiagram.com: "A Wall of Ice"
Ellipsis: "Sometimes in One's Twenties" [as "Coasting"]
The Iowa Review: "UFIs"
Stand Magazine (England): "The Blue Man," "Bright Thing Across a Bright Table," "M. Ch. Labitte"

* * * * *

A shorter version of this collection was a finalist for the 1999 Fordham University "Poets Out Loud" Award, a finalist for the 1999 Alice Faye di Castagnola Prize of the Poetry Society of America; a finalist for the 2001 *The New Criterion* Poetry Prize, and semifinalist for the 2003 Hollis Summers Poetry Prize at Ohio University Press/Swallow Press.

"History of an Ordinary Doubt" was a finalist for the 1999 Cecil Hemley Award of the Poetry Society of America.

"The Most Ordinary Thing in the World," "This One," "Raphael" and "Things That Marry" received First Honorable Mention for the 2001 Dana Award in Poetry.

"A Restlessness" (as "Zone of the Ordinary") won first prize in *The Cream City Review* 2000-2001 poetry competition.

"M. Ch. Labitte" was a finalist for *The Iowa Review* Poetry Award in 2004.

"The Blue Man," "This One," and "Bright Thing Across a Bright Table" appeared in the author's full-length collection, *Science And* (FutureCycle Press, 2014).

I particularly want to thank Diane Kistner and the editorial staff at FutureCycle Press for their enthusiasm for this project and for Diane Kistner's excellent production work.

And a special acknowledgment is due to my partner of almost forty years, poet and critic Jeredith Merrin, who made most of the visible and invisible conditions for this book possible and who critiqued uncounted iterations of each poem. I stay grateful as well, in large equal parts, for two longtime friends, Professor Helen Deutsch at UCLA and Elizabeth Brown Lockman of Green Bank, West Virginia, whose suggestions and perspectives have been invaluable.

Cover artwork, "Malvaceae: Ceiba pentandra" by Geoff Gallice; cover and interior book design by Diane Kistner; Futura text, Futura and Alexa titling

ABOUT FUTURECYCLE PRESS

FutureCycle Press is dedicated to publishing lasting English-language poetry books, chapbooks, and anthologies in both print-on-demand and Kindle ebook formats. Founded in 2007 by long-time independent editor/publishers and partners Diane Kistner and Robert S. King, the press incorporated as a non-profit in 2012. A number of our editors are distinguished poets and writers in their own right, and we have been actively involved in the small press movement going back to the early seventies.

The FutureCycle Poetry Book Prize and honorarium is awarded annually for the best full-length volume of poetry we publish in a calendar year. Introduced in 2013, our Good Works projects are anthologies devoted to issues of universal signif-icance, with all proceeds donated to a related worthy cause. Our Selected Poems series highlights contemporary poets with a substantial body of work to their credit; with this series we strive to resurrect work that has had limited distribution and is now out of print.

We are dedicated to giving all of the authors we publish the care their work deserves, making our catalog of titles the most diverse and distinguished it can be, and paying forward any earnings to fund more great books.

We've learned a few things about independent publishing over the years. We've also evolved a unique, resilient publishing model that allows us to focus mainly on vetting and preserving for posterity poetry collections of exceptional quality without becoming overwhelmed with bookkeeping and mailing, fund-raising activities, or taxing editorial and production "bubbles." To learn more about what we are doing, visit us at futurecycle.org.

THE FUTURECYCLE POETRY BOOK PRIZE

All full-length volumes of poetry published by FutureCycle Press in a given calendar year are considered for the annual FutureCycle Poetry Book Prize. This allows us to consider each submission on its own merits, outside of the context of a contest. Too, the judges see the finished book, which will have benefitted from the beautiful book design and strong editorial gloss we are famous for.

The book ranked the best in judging is announced as the prize-winner in the subsequent year. There is no fixed monetary award; instead, the winning poet receives an honorarium of 20% of the total net royalties from all poetry books and chapbooks the press sold online in the year the winning book was published. The winner is also accorded the honor of being on the panel of judges for the next year's competition; all judges receive copies of all contending books to keep for their personal library.